AF480540

LAND
by Anne Miranda

LAND

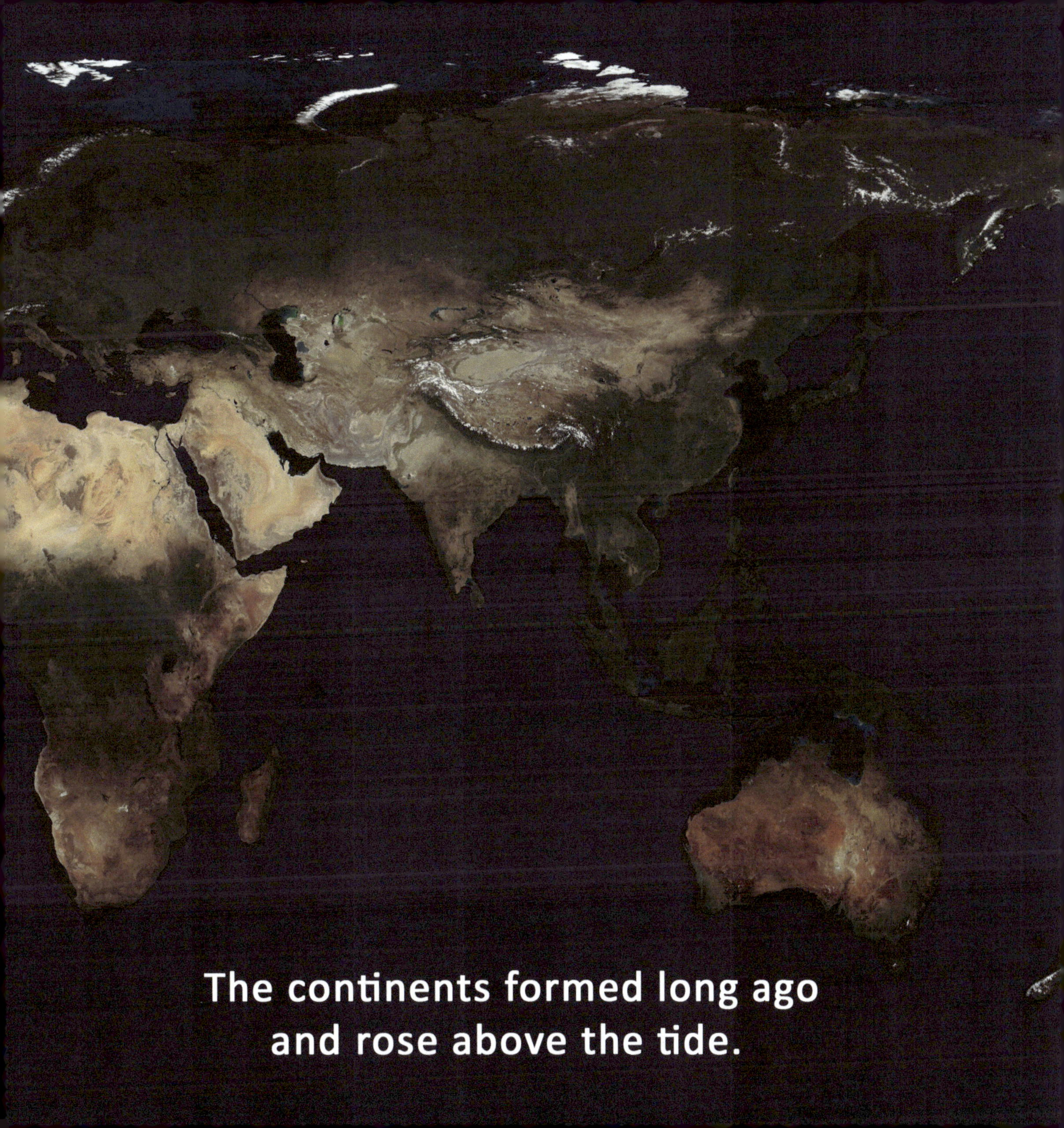

The continents formed long ago
and rose above the tide.

So things that live terrestrially
could happily abide.

Valleys, hills and mountains
wrinkle Mother Nature's skin.

Water, wind and weather
shape the land where they have been.

Volcanos spill out lava
and an earthquake causes change.

Hurricanes and glaciers,
can reform and rearrange!

Land is never idle.
It is constantly in motion...

stretching out across the plains

and dancing with the ocean.

Land is rich and fertile.

Some is buried under snow.

Desert land is arid,
and so nothing much can grow.

Land is wild and lonely

or pastoral and serene.

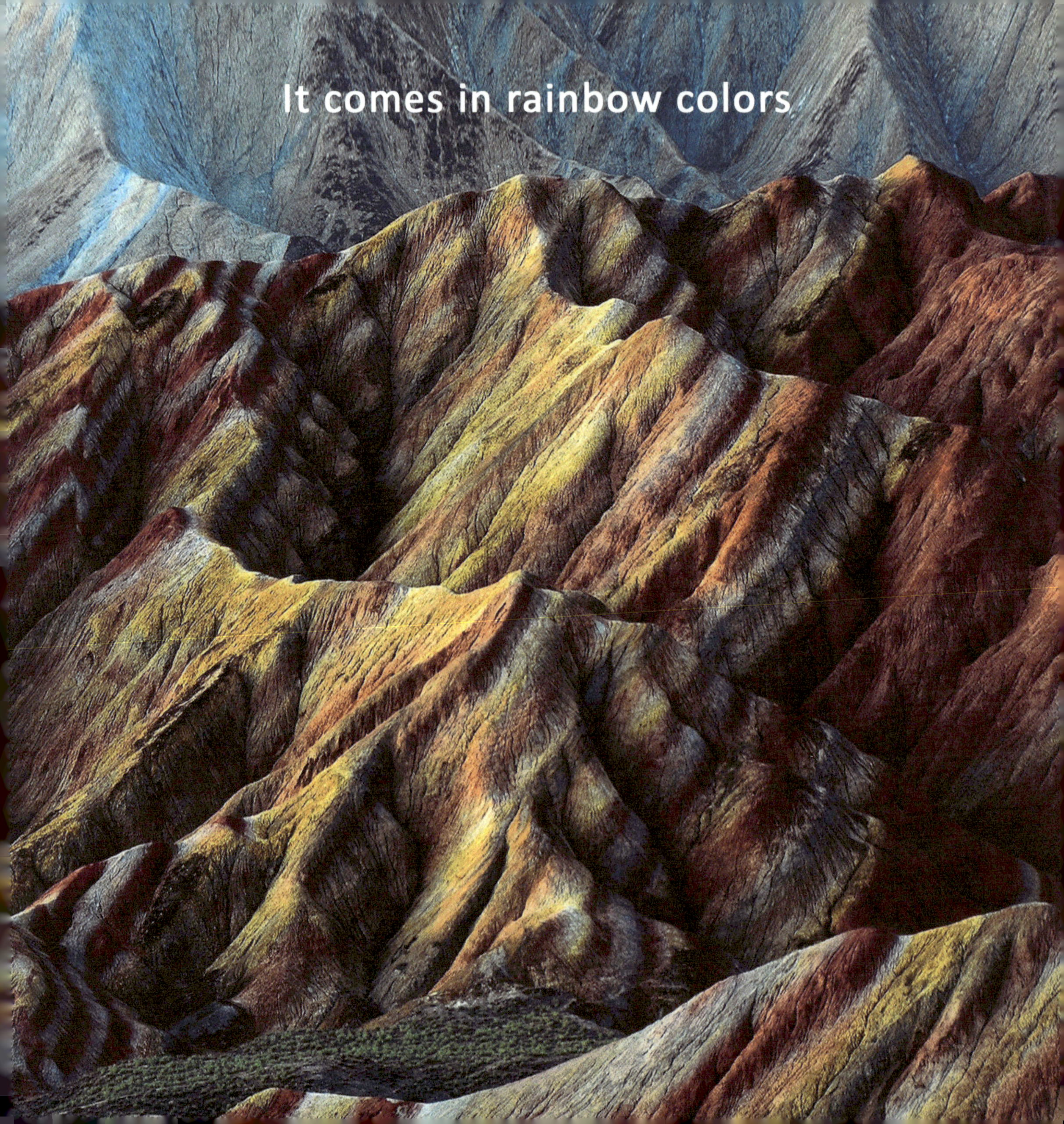

It comes in rainbow colors

or in hues of grassy green.

It's shaded by the forests

and it shimmers in the light.

It's covered by the jungle

and with gardens that delight!

The ground on which we're standing
is our one and only home –

where people build their dwellings

and where herds of bison roam.

The land is good for burrows,
digging warrens, holes and lairs.

Cliffs are right for nesting birds

and caves for sleepy bears.

The earth is quite spectacular
when seen from high above.

Wherever you are living
there is land that you should love.

Explore the world around you.
There's so much for you to do!

Climb a hill and hike a trail.

Be still, enjoy the view.

Use our planet wisely
and treat every inch with care.

Celebrate this precious land
we all are meant to share.

Book design by Tyler Miranda

Many thanks to the photographers on
www.pixabay.com for their beautiful images.